THE ULTIMATE GUIDE

HOW TO WIN BACK YOUR EX

TABLE OF CONTENTS

PREFACE

There are countless reasons why relationships fall apart, perhaps you're one who screwed up or you made a mistake? Or maybe your ex is to blame, but you still want to give things another go!
Possibly she's with someone new, and you want to win her back! It doesn't matter, because the information within this book, you'll discover methods and techniques that are psychologically proven to get your ex back.

You won't find these techniques or methods from your relationship self-help guide from your generic bookstore. You wouldn't even get them from any marriage counsellor. Why? because the material within is very contrary to the traditional advice you've ever been given before.

Despite this, you must realize everything recommended actually works. It is based on female psychology and scientific principals. Never forget that.

That being said like any book, this is only as good as the action you back it with. In other words, you need to apply what you learn. Fortunately for you, the vast majority of what you are about to learn is actually pretty easy stuff.

INTRODUCTION

omen have always been an enigma to us men. Their actions and behaviours often seem so damn illogical and confusing.

It's true that some of a woman's behaviour can be attributed to PMS, but there's actually much more going on than just PMS and a headache. Women, just like us men, are biologically programmed through millions of years of evolution to behave in very specific ways. To women, the attraction is a lot like a bunch of light switches. Flick on enough of them and you'll have to beat them off you with a stick

What you'll learn within this book are techniques that will teach you exactly how to flick those switches, so that you can win back your ex-girlfriend or wife.

In fact, the techniques and strategies in this book are so productive that not only will you have no problem winning them back, but also in keeping control of the relationship.

That being said, like everything of importance, the power contained in these pages can be utilized for both good and evil. I leave it to you, the reader, to be mature enough to utilize this information for your own motivations behind it.

We have intentionally made sure to keep this book within a 70-page limit, for your convenience. Why? Because we don't believe in adding "fluff" just to increase the page count, like so many other traditional authors, do. You'll find everything that needs to be explained to be in depth and leave out the irrelevant fluff.

Once you've read this, you might want to check out the next

step to our relationship guides "The Ultimate Guide - How To
Train Your Girlfriend" It's jam-packed with more insight
into the female mind. You'll find practical, meaty advice on
what to do when in a relationship so your girlfriend will never
dump you again. There are very specific things most all men
do when in a relationship that almost guarantees the woman
he is with will lose attraction for him.

The "How To Train Your Girlfriend" book will explain to
you exactly what things you did to cause your ex to no longer
feel attraction for you. And make no mistake - that is the core
reason she broke up with you: a loss of attraction. It further
goes on to give practical advice on what things you must do
to maintain attraction. I promise you it will be one
of the most useful best books, you've ever read.

A LESSON ON FEMALES

Want to know the real reason your girlfriend broke up with you? Want to know the secret women will never let men in on? Start getting excited because most men will go to their graves not knowing this stuff.

First, you must come to realize that your ex-girlfriend was not originally attracted to you by chance. There were strong physiological factors at work which facilitated her attraction toward you. Attraction is not a conscious choice for women (or men for that matter). Your girlfriend was attracted to how you behaved and eventually lost attraction for you based on how you behaved (again). Like most all men, you eventually stopped displaying the specific traits that women are so drawn to.

You see, while men are mostly attracted to a woman's physical beauty, a woman is, for the most part, attracted to a man's behaviour. There are specific traits men exhibit which attract women to them like crazy. You, at one time, exhibited some of these traits (without even realizing it) to attract your ex-girlfriend. As your relationship progressed, you lost some, most or all of these attractive traits and replaced them with unattractive ones.

"Aha!"

What I'm about to teach you has much broader implications than just getting your ex back. You'll be able to consciously influence any woman's attraction for you on a much, much more conscious level. I'd say a good 95% of men have no clue how to behave around women (in an attractive way). You're about to enter the realm of the elite 5%.

UNATTRACTIVE TRAITS

Let's first discuss unattractive traits. These are the traits you began to display over the span of your relationship. These are the core reasons your girlfriend broke up with you, even if she played it off as something else. In the vast majority of cases, women themselves do not even understand why they suddenly lose attraction for their boyfriend or even husband. It just happens and they don't consciously know why. But I do…

INSECURITY

Say hello to the #1 killer of attraction. Women are just as repelled by an insecure man as men are repelled by Rosie O'Donnell. And I'm not even joking!

Insecurity will manifest itself in many, many different forms. Most of which we will discuss below.

ACTING JEALOUS

The jealous boyfriend is a very unattractive boyfriend indeed. Jealousy absolutely reeks of insecurity. It says "I feel threatened by other men because deep down I don't view myself as worthy of you". Women are not attracted to a man who constantly acts jealous toward other guys because it demonstrates weakness on his part.

These types of jealous guys will ask their girlfriends who they are with all the time, get pissed off when their girlfriend talks to other men or even hang out with them. They will often make fun of other men their girlfriend is friends with just to look "cool". In reality, this type of behaviour only makes them look ridiculously insecure.

You need to assume the attitude "other men just make me look good" and leave her to talk to whoever the heck she wants because, in the end, you'll only look better.

BEING CONTROLLING

Putting handcuffs on and controlling your girlfriend only further shows insecurity. Men will often demand their girlfriend not hang out with other men or even their own friends.

A man is controlling because deep down he feels as though he is not good enough for his girlfriend. He thinks he must control her in order for her to stay with him. Ironically, the tighter he closes his fist, the further she will slip through his fingers.

It is human nature to rebel against that which attempts to control us. Much like when we are children, we rebel against our parents for limiting our behaviour.

"PEDESTALING" & NOT VALUING YOURSELF

Women want a man who will value himself just as much as he values her. The minute you put your girlfriend on a pedestal and start placing her needs ahead of your own is the minute she will leave you. She will lose all respect for you and move on to a man who values himself just as much as he values her.

I hear about guys acting all needy and insecure like this constantly. They like what their girlfriend likes. They do what their girlfriend wants to do.   They basically place their girlfriend on a pedestal and say "I value you more then I value myself". Totally not attractive.

Women want a man who values himself just as much as he values her. No exceptions.

"He who cares least controls the relationship"

Ever wonder why women are so drawn to jerks? Well, this is largely the reason. Women are attracted to the fact they value themselves so much. While this doesn't mean you should become a jerk, you should adopt their positive attitude toward themselves.

BEING APPROVAL SEEKING

Looking to your girlfriend for her approval on everything is insecure. Being externally validation driven is the hallmark of an insecure, low self-esteem man.

Do any of the following sound familiar?

> Do you really like me?
> Do you think my penis is big?
> What would you rate me on a scale of
> 1 – 10? Did you have a good time with
> me tonight? Do you like this shirt?
> How good am I in bed?

The list could go on for the entire length of this book but I'll spare you the unnecessary drivel. Work on understanding what it means to be approval seeking and think about how you could have been approval seeking while in your relationship.

BEING CLINGY

> Spending too much time together is not a good thing. Diamonds are valuable because they are rare. If you could just walk outside your house and pick up a diamond, you wouldn't pay a jeweller a ton of money for it. I mean, that's just common sense.

> Despite the fact that may be common sense, most people don't think to consider its social implications. It applies to people perfectly. Stop and consider whether or not you started acting clingy toward the end of your relationship, right before your ex broke up with you.

DOMINANT TRAITS

Just as there are particular behaviours men display that repel women, there are dominant traits that attract them in droves. First of all, the
very fact that you are reading this tells me a few things:

> You're attracted to women. Since you had a girlfriend, you are to some degree a dominant male yourself. You would not have been able to attract a woman for a long-term relationship
> had you not been. This makes my job a lot easier.

> You take charge and correct things that go wrong in your life. You bought this eBook and that alone tells me you possess a number of attractive traits.

The dominant traits that attract women are as follows:

LEADERSHIP

Actively taking the lead and having a plan is of paramount importance. Has your girlfriend ever asked you something along the lines of "what do you want to do tonight?" and you replied with "I don't know, what do you want to do?" Well, we have a problem with that, as it demonstrates a lack of leadership. Remember that women are biologically attracted to a specific type of man. It is hardcoded in their DNA.

Every time you fail to have a plan, she loses attraction for you. Your role, based on millions of years of human evolution, dictates that you should be the one leading your girlfriend, while she follows your lead. Embrace this.

CONFIDENCE

We all know that women are for some reason attracted to jerks. Well, confidence plays a huge part in that. Remember that it is

not the jerk they are attracted to, but rather the specific traits he displays. Confidence is certainly one of those traits.

It is important that you not confuse confidence with arrogance. Arrogance is a sort of fake confidence and it's pretty obvious and transparent. Women can smell fake confidence a million miles away. It is not enough to fake your confidence, you must actually possess it.

SELF-ASSURANCE

Women do not want a doormat-man. You need to be assured of your own opinions and beliefs. I see a lot of guys compromising their own values because they think that if they do, their girlfriend will like them more. They will change their taste in music, clothes, activities, etc, etc. Women don't want a puppy dog, they want a man with his own opinions, values and beliefs.

PURPOSE

A man who is driven by a purpose is an unbelievable powerful "attraction switch". We men don't so much care if the women in your lives have lots of ambition.

If a woman demonstrates power and ambition were not going to be either turned on by it (in the vast majority of cases). In fact, it will probably threaten us and indeed turn us off.

Somewhere along the path of your relationship, you may have lost focus with your life. You lost your purpose, or indeed your girlfriend became your purpose.

In this day and age, it's extremely hard for a man to have a strong focus and purpose with his life. It's truly sad, yet so common.

So you might be asking yourself, "what exactly would you consider a purpose?" Well, it's certainly not routinely going to work each morning, coming home, eating, playing video games and going to bed. Mundane routine is the anti-purpose.

The following are a list of things myself as well as thousands of my past students have focused on, to give their lives purpose:

Training for an upcoming marathon.

Striving for financial freedom.

Working out with the goal of weight loss and "getting ripped" in mind.

Focusing on getting a record deal or just getting an album recorded.

Pursuing any kind of sport.

Pursuing anything at all that gives you passion and excitement.

Men who flail about life with no real purpose or reason for being there are not very attractive. Especially when (like most men, and like you probably did) you made your girlfriend your purpose. When this happens, a breakup will soon ensue. Women do not want a boyfriend whose sole purpose in life is to please her.

It's a major turn off. Instant attraction death. Don't blame women for this, because it is how they are programmed to behave, feel and react. There is no conscious choice in the matter.

MALE/FEMALE POLARITY

The men of today are missing something special. Something we used to have up until recently. We men are slowly becoming more and more feminine while women are becoming more and more masculine. Women are genetically pre-programmed to mate with a dominant male. Accept this.

Regardless of how far our society has progressed or how self-aware the human species has become, there will always be an underlying animal instinct driving us along. Women will always be attracted to a masculine, dominant man. Always.

Women do <u>not</u> want the power in a relationship.

I can hear Oprah crying right now, as I type this. No matter what women say or how many feminists take over the world, this will remain true. As sexist as it may first appear, I 100% know it to be true. Women do not want to be in a relationship that they control and call all the shots. They want the man to be the one holding all the cards, so to speak.

"He who cares least controls the relationship"

That sentence is worth quoting again because of its implications for your situation. You see, right now your ex-girlfriend holds all the power. She cares least. She's not the one reading an eBook on how to get you back. Know this and accept it. You need to first understand it in order for us to later work on techniques to reverse it.

BEFORE AND AFTER SHOT

Imagine, if you will, a before and after shot of the man you were and the man you eventually became. When you first started dating your ex, you were confident, playful and flirtatious. You were secure in yourself and probably held all the power. If you're anything like 95% of most guys, you slowly started to change.

Gradually, you began to act more and more controlling, jealous, needy and weak. The male/female polarity started to shift. Your girlfriend began to take on the dominant role while you became increasingly submissive. At around this point, your girlfriends pre-programming kicked in (it's not her fault) and she began to see you as unattractive.

It's a lot like a woman who lets herself get fat and then calls her boyfriend shallow for leaving her. Her boyfriend wasn't shallow; his pre-programming kicked in and caused him to lose attraction. It's in his genetic code to seek out a specific type of shape: a specific hip to waist ratio, facial symmetry, etc, etc.

The same applies to women and insecure men. An insecure man is a fat woman. He's not at all attractive. In a sense, you let yourself get fat with insecurity which is what caused your ex to lose attraction
for you

NO CONTACT

D oes that title scare you? If so, you above all others must pay particularly close attention to the next few paragraphs.

There is no point in me sugar coating my words and tiptoeing around my point so I'm just going to blurt it out:

DO NOT INITIATE CONTACT WITH YOUR EX-GIRLFRIEND FOR A MINIMUM OF FOUR WEEKS.

There are no exceptions to this rule. You must not be the one to initiate contact with her, but it is perfectly fine if she contact you first. There is a scientific, physiological basis for this and I will explain it shortly. It will all make sense and you'll have one of those "aha!" moments. A-freakin' light bulb will appear over your head. Swear to God.

Why the need to not initiate contact with your ex-girlfriend?

The "no contact rule" is a mechanism we use to accomplish three things:

1. It prevents you from acting needy and insecure around your ex-girlfriend. As you already discovered, neediness and insecurity are attraction death when it comes to women.

2. It instils a fear of loss within her. Not contacting her pushes her away and makes her wonder why. She will essentially become intrigued and start wondering if you have moved on with another woman. Humans only realize something's value when it is gone, in most cases.

3. It gives you the opportunity to soak in as much information from my material as possible.

You see, no matter what you do or how hard you try, when you're around your ex-girlfriend you will sub-communicate insecurity and neediness. At least at first, you will. It doesn't even matter how hard you try not to; it will come through in some way or another.

Women (much more so than men) are incredibly good at picking up on non-verbal emotions. So even if you don't verbally say you miss your girlfriend and want her back or that you're hurting inside, she will pick up on your feelings through your body language. That's not a bunch of BS crap either. Body language is powerful stuff.

Much of this eBook will be about both actually ridding yourself of insecurity and neediness as well as some tricks and gimmicks to make yourself appear a lot less insecure and needy than you really are. Even if you feel horrible inside, I will at least give you the appearance that you are doing perfectly fine.

DONT BE HER EMOTIONAL TAMPON

After a breakup, women use their ex-boyfriend as a means to get over the breakup and heal themselves. By not contacting her and making yourself scarce, you are forcing her to heal on her own. You won't be around to support her and be all sensitive. You are forcing her to be lonely and face reality without you. There will be no easing out of being in a relationship with you.

Your instincts may tell you that by being around her and supporting her (emotionally) will only draw you back together.

Nothing could be any further from the truth. This will only help her healing process while hurting yours. Essentially she will unintentionally be leeching off you. I guess you could even consider her an emotional vampire: sucking the happiness from you and substituting it with jealousy, hurt and shame.

IF SHE CONTACTS YOU

It's very likely that your ex-girlfriend will actually initiate contact with you over the course of these 30 days, provided you follow my plan exactly as outlined. This is especially true if she starts really feeling a fear of loss and begins to place value on you once again. It will
be her natural instinct to reach out and contact you.

This is a very good sign and while not at all necessary, definitely will make things a lot easier for you at later stages of this plan.

Rule number one here is not to be rude, angry or act depressed around her. If she comes in to visit you at work or calls you on the phone, act happy and cheerful. Acting in this manner will demonstrate higher value on your part. Basically, she will wonder why you're not acting miserable and rotten. This will intrigue her and again make her feel an even stronger fear of loss (as you appear to have moved on before her).

When your ex contacts you:

    Make small talk with her about whatever.

    Let her lead the conversation.

    Act cheerful and happy but don't come across as desperate to talk with her.

    End the conversation first (if it's a phone call) after about 10 minutes. Be polite and say "I'm heading out with a friend but I'll give you a call later". Make sure you don't come across as bitter when you say this.

Take your time to call her back. Don't be too eager and make sure you wait for a day or a day and a half.

If you run into her in person, make small talk for 10 minutes and then say something along the lines of, "Well it was nice talking with you, but I have to finish doing __________." Again, be cheerful about it. Being cheerful demonstrates security.

The "no contact rule" doesn't mean your ex-girlfriend can't contact you. It's a very good thing when she is the one initiating contact first, but only if she is the one doing the initiating. The important thing to remember is that under no circumstances will you be the one initiating contact with her.

What **NOT** to do in a nutshell:

Act angry.

Act depressed and sad.

Act rude and treat her like crap.

Brag about how many women you're sleeping with or dating. (This will obviously come across as a lie and make you look like a loser)

Bring up anything about the relationship at all.

Ask if she's dating or sleeping with anyone.

Ask/beg her to give the relationship "another shot".

It's very likely that over the next few weeks, your ex will contact you. In fact, many of my students have only applied the No Contact principal and have experienced dramatic success with it. This is largely due to the fact No Contact forces your ex to realize your value. You can't value something that's always been there to its fullest extent.

Again, I'd like to reiterate that it is important that you act rather cheerful, cool, calm and collected when she contacts you. No acting depressed! Period.

Let the conversation unfold and basically talk about positive things that have nothing to do with your relationship. Let her lead the conversation and do most of the talking. If she brings up anything about the relationship then it's safe to enter into that line of discussion. As
long as you're not the one bringing it up, you're A-OK.

I can't even tell you how many times I've heard from guys who followed the No Contact rule and had their ex girlfriends call them weeks later, asking if they would give the relationship another shot. All they did was sit around on their butts and not initiate contact with their ex's.

Three Weeks = Peak of Loneliness

The "loneliness peak" occurs after about three to four weeks. She will feel her most vulnerable and lonely at this time. It will take great effort on her part not to contact you. In most cases, provided you stick to the rest of this plan, she will be the one contacting you. If she doesn't then that's still fine, but you will be in a much better position if she is the one initiating contact with you.

After three to four weeks have passed, it will be much more effective for you to contact her at this point. She will be lonely and most likely thinking good thoughts about you. She will be reminiscing about the good times you had together while you'll be concentrating on only the bad. The balance of power will have turned and she will be the insecure one while you're not.

If She Does Not Contact You...

Since the loneliness peak occurs at three to four weeks, it is safe for you to contact her at this point. In the majority of cases she will contact you first. If not, I recommend waiting a minimum of three to four weeks. This really depends on how needy and insecure you were acting before the breakup. In extreme cases, you should wait even longer.

If you have to contact her, you will chat with her as though she is an old friend. Again, I reiterate that there is to be no hint of desperation, depression or neediness on your part. You must come across as though you are perfectly fine with the breakup. Act like you realized the breakup was actually the best thing for the both of you.

I recommend that you tell her, when you initiate contact, that you believe the breakup was definitely for the best and that it would be a shame to throw away such a great friendship.

"I just wanted to tell you that you were right... The breakup was definitely for the best. It would really be a shame to throw away our friendship though. How about we go out for a coffee bud? We can work on being friends again, no hard feelings."

It's very important that you maintain a platonic vibe of being friends. Again, this is to instil a fear of loss within her. Remember that we value most that which we do not have. I will talk more about the importance of the platonic friend vibe later on. Regardless of whether she contacts you or you have to contact her, you will use your friendship as a means to sneak in and present to her the new, confident, less needy you to her. You will use your position as a friend to rebuild attraction.

Some Possible Objections

So what if you're in a situation where you cannot possibly "not contact" your ex girlfriend? Maybe you work with her, you have a kid with her, you live together, etc. What the heck do you do then?

Basically, it's all about how you behave in these circumstances. You don't want to come across as insecure or childish by acting angry, jealous or all out ignoring her. However, you do want to keep contact with your ex to a minimum.

If you live together, make sure you go out with friends a lot. Don't bring other women back to the house just to make her jealous since this will probably hurt your chances of getting her back. She'll end up bringing a guy back and it'll end up turning into a vicious cycle of games. Stay away from that.

Basically, you want your ex to initiate the conversation most of the time. You don't want to look like you're ignoring her because that's also insecure. You want to act happy and cheerful like you're completely fine with the breakup and you have moved on. Let her lead the conversation and put in most of the work when conversing with you. Again, don't ignore her; just let her do most of the work.

PUSH-PULL THEORY

Push/Pull theory revolves around the notion that we want what we cannot have. We pursue that which retreats from us. It's true for both men and women alike. In fact, the main reason you want your ex back so badly is probably due to the fact she rejected you. You currently cannot have her and that drives you insane. It would drive me insane too. That's just human nature.

People interact in two basic ways (when you really break it down). We are either pushing somebody away from us, or we are pulling them toward us. To "pull" is to show interest and to "push" is to show disinterest.

When somebody (like a women) pushes us away, we naturally respond by pulling that person back in. It creates a fear of loss and we naturally want to vanquish that fear and fill the gap. This is especially true with male/female romantic relationships.

A push can be anything from your girlfriend saying "I need more space" or "you're being annoying" or outright breaking up with you. It is anything she does to display disinterest or indifference.

"He who cares least controls the relationship"

Right now, you instinctively want to pull your ex-girlfriend toward you when in fact you should be pushing her away from you. Pulling her toward you puts pressure on her and forces her to push you further away. If she knows she can have you whenever she wants, she won't want you at all. It will kill all the sexual tension between the two of you.

I've already presented you with one very powerful technique that harnesses Push/Pull Theory. By not initiating contact with your ex, she will begin to wonder if you have moved on. She will probably start to think about all the good times you had together and crave to have those times back. Remember that after 3 – 4 weeks, her loneliness will peak.

It's also important to realize that just as you can "pull" too much, you can also push too much as well. Sexual tension is created when there is a mix of the two. You will often hear women refer to this as "mixed signals". They'll say things like "he was sending mixed signals and it just made me want him more".

The key to push/pull is to find the right balance. Push her away from you a little and then pull her back in, push her away from a little once again, then pull her back in.

Now, I'm a professional "pickup artist", so I have the art of push/pull mastered. You're just trying to get your ex back and so you really don't have to put too much thought into it. Just make sure you understand that too much of either pushing or pulling is bad. You want to show some interest, then show a little disinterest. Rinse and repeat.

LETTING GO

our internal mindset is of paramount importance when applying these techniques. You need to rid yourself of any and all insecurity for this to work. If you're serious about getting your ex-girlfriend back, following this plan will be easy. This next part will be very counter intuitive but I can assure you that it is based on deep-rooted psychology.

Accept that things are over and begin the process of moving on.

Yup. That's right. You need to let go of your ex-girlfriend before you can get her back. Very counter-intuitive indeed. You need to remember that a needy, insecure guy repels women like no other. Letting go (and I do actually mean really letting go) will dramatically increase the odds of getting her back merely because it rids you of any and all approval seeking behaviour. The following are not useless steps to be ignored. Man-up and follow them.

Step One: Go grab a piece of paper right now (its best you do it while you're reading this). Write out your ex-girlfriends contact information on it and set it aside. Place it in a spot where you will not easily see it.

Step Two: Delete every memory and mode of contact you have with her. Delete her number from your phone, delete her from Text Messengers, WhatsApp, Snapchat, Skype or whatever other instant messaging system you use. Delete all of her e-mails (that means to stop reading them too).

The only exception to this rule is on Facebook. If you don't have an account (or she doesn't) then don't worry. If you do, leave her on your list but do not, under any circumstances, view her profile. I cannot stress this enough. There is to be absolutely no viewing of her profile!

To recap:

Delete all modes of contact: phone number, Facebook WhatsApp, email, etc.
Delete digital photos.
Delete anything else that reminds you of her.

Do not ever view her online profile.

Step Three: Gather up all physical reminders of your ex girlfriend. This means any teddy bears, cards, posters, clothes, watches, <u>pictures</u>, etc. Anything physical at all! Gather it all up and toss it in a box. Make sure you put the box in a place you cannot find. Put it in your basement or leave it with a friend or something. Under your bed will not suffice.

Step Four: Visualize yourself with other women. Fantasize about other women. Under no circumstances should you let your mind drift and begin to think about your ex in a sexual way. When you find yourself thinking about your ex, force yourself to fantasize about an even more beautiful women. It's also helpful to fantasize about what you would do with a million dollars or something equally pleasurable.

Realize that you're fantasizing about your ex to help comfort and ease the pain for yourself. It will only have the opposite effect which is why you must force yourself to let go. In a week or two, the pain will have dramatically decreased.

Step Five: Concentrate only on the negative aspects of your ex-girlfriend. When going through a breakup, we have what's called selective memory. We only seem to remember the good times we had with them and how happy they made us. Your ex-girlfriend becomes a sort of drug that we withdraw from. It's hard, but you must only focus on the negative.

TAKING YOUR LIFE BACK

Here is where it gets interesting. By getting your life back, you are showing your ex-girlfriend you do not need her. Remember: women do not want a man who needs her more than she needs him. They want an independent man with his own sense of reality. They want you to hold the keys.

By actively demonstrating that you are healing and moving on, you will begin to switch on many of those attraction switches we talked about earlier. These are the same switches (dominant traits) that attracted her in the first place. It's your job to demonstrate you still have those characteristics.

Start Dating Other Women

This is my favourite technique for moving on. Actually moving on! You don't need to actually be serious about these dates, but they will be a huge confidence boost for your ego and will really help shed any underlying insecurity and/or neediness.

I realize you may not be in the dating frame of mind but you must force yourself to do it. You must force yourself to find other women to date. Like much of what we have discussed thus far, this is also very counter-intuitive, so allow me to explain:

> Dating other women builds your confidence (women love confidence) while simultaneously shedding any underlying insecurity you may still have.

> When your ex-girlfriend finds out, she will feel the fear of loss. Her sub-conscious will be thinking, "wow, he must be more high value than I thought if he can replace me that easily".

So with that said, go ask that cutie in accounting out or the hotty at the coffee shop. You'll seriously love yourself for it later. This sounds like "feel good" advice but there are seriously millions of hot, datable women out there. At the moment, you're very emotional and you're not thinking logically. You're an attractive guy and it won't be overly
difficult for you to move on if you so desire.

Now, if all else fails and you cannot actually get on some dates within the next week or two, then it's appropriate to fake it. You can even start off by faking it until you actually get on a few real dates too. The important thing is that you try to go on some real, actual dates and make sure your ex girlfriend finds out about it. It'll do wonders for your hurt self-esteem.

Techniques to make sure she finds out:

Instant Messaging Hang Out

Chances are you use an online instant messaging system like WhatsApp, Instagram, Skype or Snapchat. Usually, people mention what they are doing in their display name. For example:

"John - At Phil's Tonight… Call my phone." Where I live, this is very common.

If you land a date (don't be picky either) make sure your display name mentions the fact you are out with another woman. For example: "John – Out with Tiff. Back tonight." You see what we're doing? We're creating what's called a jealousy plotline to increase your perceived value while making your ex feel the fear of loss.

If you can't actually get on a date, fake it if you must. Make up a random women's name and say you're "Out with Tiff" or Jill or whoever. Whatever you do, do not make it look like you're intentionally trying to make your ex jealous. This would be a mistake of paramount disaster. You need to allude to the fact you are moving on with your life and

seeing other women. She can't think it's all a game you're playing to make her want you
back.

Allude To Her Friend

Chances are you talk to somebody your ex-girlfriend hangs out with on a regular basis. Get yourself in a casual conversation with them and ask what they're up to this weekend. When they finish telling you, you know they will reciprocate and ask you the exact same question.

When they ask what you're doing, say "I'm just hanging out with some Jill girl I met the other night." Then quickly change the topic! Do not directly say "yeah so I'm going on a date tonight" as that would just make you look like a loser who wants his ex to get jealous. Make it look like you almost don't want their friend knowing you're going on a date but it just slipped out.

Social Site Flirting

These days, everyone has a Facebook account (or some other variation thereof). Maybe you don't and if so ignore this info. If you do, read on.

Take this opportunity to flirt with other women in your network. Just message them, talk with them, etc. The great thing about Facebook is that they have public sections where people can post messages back and forth to each other. Everyone in your friend's list can read these messages and you can bet your ex-girlfriend will be viewing your profile to keep tabs on what you have been up to. Especially since you're not initiating contact with her.

Again, this will create a jealousy plotline. She'll see that you are attractive to other women and feel the fear of loss. Even though she broke up with you, she's used to

feeling as though she owns you. She's used to having you all to herself. When she sees other women flirting with you on your profile, she'll
get jealous and realize what a horrible mistake she's made.

Social Site Fake Out

You can take things a step further and register another account, under a fake female name. Put up a fake picture of a very pretty girl. Make sure the picture doesn't look blatantly fake either. If it's a celebrity or a women way out of your league, forget about it appearing genuine. For best effect, make it a woman just slightly better looking than your ex-girlfriend.

Anyway, set the fake profile to private. I'll say that again because it's so damn important. Set the fake profile to private so nobody can actually view it. You will look like a huge loser when your ex views the fake profile only to find out it's completely empty and clearly a phoney profile designed to make her jealous.

Next, make a few posts from the fake account to your own account saying things like "great movie – we'll have to do it again" or "you're too funny! We'll have to chill again on Sunday."

Basically, you want it to look like you may possibly be dating another pretty girl. Definitely, do not post anything blatantly sexual like "you have a huge dick" or something equally as lame. Keep it very subtle and make sure you describe the way you type. You probably abbreviate certain words, use specific slang, spell certain words wrong and other identifiable patterns that may give away the fact the phoney mystery girl if actually you. Pay attention to the way you type and make sure it's different when using this technique.

Remember that none of those techniques are actually necessary. I recommend them because:

Your ex will fear she is losing you for good. It knocks her back into reality.

She will be overwhelmed with jealousy if you played your cards correctly.

It demonstrates higher value on your part.

It builds your own self-confidence back up and increases your self-esteem.

The major benefit will come from actually going on real dates because it will rocket your self-confidence. You will believe in your own attractiveness again. That's not something you can achieve through faking it. Although if you absolutely have to, the option is there. Just make sure you do it in a subtle way that doesn't come across as bragging. Only losers brag.

Secondly, I want you to use your imagination and come up with other creative ways in which you can subtly allude to being on dates with other women. I gave you a lot of great examples to get you started. Just make sure you do not go over the top and make yourself look like a loser by bragging and generally making it obvious you are trying to make her jealous.

Start Having Massive Fun

Next, on our list of getting back, your ex-girlfriend is to demonstrate that you are now having massive fun. You want to make her regret she ever left you. She'll even start to think she was the one holding you back from experiencing your life. And who knows, maybe she actually was.

Go out and start having some fun with your friends. Have some drinks with the guys next weekend, hit up a bar or club, get that adrenaline pumping. Hell, you should even go on that trip you always wanted to take. Just go and have as much fun as you possibly can.

This will:

Rid you of your needy, insecure mindset.

Demonstrate to your ex-girlfriend that you will not sit around wallowing in your own sorrow.

Keep your mind off your ex (which ties in with ridding yourself of insecurity)

The number one thing I recommend you do is to start working out. Sign up at the gym and work your ass off for the next month. Not because you think you have to, but because you will enjoy it.

Exercise releases endorphins which basically make you feel good. This is a scientifically proven fact. Working out will release a lot of endorphins.

Working out boosts your testosterone level. Testosterone actually increases your confidence which women are very attracted to.

It will keep your mind occupied and off your ex-girlfriend.

You'll be more physically attractive and fit.

There are many other things you can do besides working out. You can always submerse yourself into a hobby or something you've always wanted to take up. Personally, I love to learn about something new when I'm feeling troubled.

I strongly recommend you take this as an opportunity to kick back and learn all you can about female psychology and basically what women are attracted to in a man. If you're anything like me, you'll find it extremely fascinating (not to mention useful).

Just remember that if you sit around feeling sorry for yourself all day, that will just be proof in your ex girlfriends eyes that you actually were a loser and that she was completely justified in dumping you. She expects you to sit around and wallow in your own miserable pity. That is how we are expected to act after a breakup. You will be different. You will be cheerful and happy.

You must take on the mindset that: although you cared about your ex-girlfriend, this breakup is not the end of the world and possibly even a good thing.

Women don't get back together with guys that sit around feeling sorry for themselves. Women are strange creatures. They want to get back together with the guys who move on faster than they do. They start to doubt themselves and wonder why you're getting over them so fast. And then, as you're seemingly pushing them away, enjoying your life, they instinctively react by pulling you back in.

You push, they pull.

Before you know it, you will have turned the tables and your ex-girlfriend will be your ex no longer. She will have come crawling back to you as you will have proven your inner strength as a man.

Take Lots of Pictures

While you're having massive amounts of fun and adventure, make sure to take lots of pictures. Digital pictures if you can.

When you have these pictures of yourself and friends, make sure to post them as display pics on your online profiles Snapchat, Instagram. You can also post them on Facebook; basically, any social networking site you and your ex both frequent.

Seeing pictures of you and your friend having a great time will display higher value on your part while making her remember all the good times you both had together. Trust me when I say this tactic works very well.

IF SHES ALREADY DATING

So what if your ex-girlfriend is already going on dates with other guys or even seeing one guy in particular? Well, first of all, I wouldn't worry too much. These rebounds almost never work out. She's using this other guy (or guys) as a means to comfort herself and ease the pain of the breakup. Women are known for having multiple replacement guys waiting in line. These replacements are never high-quality guys and thus you have little to worry about in that department.

With that in mind, you need to be completely cool about it. Speaking from personal experience here, when one of my exes called me up (after not contacting her for a week) she immediately tried to make me jealous by alluding to a guy she was going on a date with. The funny thing is that what I'm teaching you, women almost instinctively know already. They do all this stuff by instinct alone.

Anyway, when she started going on about how she was going on a date I was completely cool about it. I didn't even have to act because deep down I knew the only reason she was telling me was to make me jealous. I told her I thought it was awesome and changed the subject. I didn't act bitter, angry or hurt. I just played it off like it was nothing.

If You Run Into Them Together

So what if you just happen to actually meet the new guy she is dating? If you've read every word up until this point, I'm sure you already
have a good idea what to do already. Act cool about it.

Don't show jealousy.

Don't show anger.

Don't ignore him.

Don't put him down or act rude.

You need to pretty much do the opposite of the above. You need to act cheerful and happy to see them both. Shake his hand, give him a pat on the back and wink while saying, "Careful, she bites" with a big smile on your face. Continue to make cheerful small talk and then excuse yourself. You need to act totally secure, calm and cool about the fact she's with another guy.

Sure you'll be dying on the inside but you have to do everything you can to repress those insecure feelings. You can't let them manifest themselves on the outside. The cooler you act, the more frustrated your ex will become.

The guy she's with will end up feeling threatened by your calm confidence.

LOOKING GOOD

lright stud muffin, it's your time to freshen up. Even if you've already got style, it's still important to look "fresh". Basically, you want to look new in her eyes, for when you eventually meet up and catch up on "old times". You don't want her looking at the old you, as it will remind her of negative things. New is completely neutral and unexplored. It's exciting.

(NOTE: Did you know that if things start getting sexually boring in a relationship, you just have to both dress up in completely different clothes and maybe even put on a wig for the lust to come back? The minute I had my girlfriend put on a blue wig I wanted to jump on her. Seriously. The same psychological principal applies to what I am recommending here.)

I've already mentioned that working out will do loads of good for you. It'll increase your confidence, make you look better and make you feel great. That all goes without saying. I urge you to work on that first.

Now we can talk about a fresh new look for you. You want her thinking "wow, what am I missing out on". It's also important to realize that I'm not asking you to totally change the way you dress/look. I'd never ask you to change who you are for a woman. Women want a man who is true to himself. I'm asking you to buy some new clothes and even get a new haircut. The purpose is to look fresh (ie: new).

This is a powerful physiological "trick" and I strongly urge you take it seriously. New clothes, new look. Do it as soon as you can. It also has the added benefit of making you feel much more confident. When you put on new clothes that make you feel good, you automatically have a rush of confidence. I recommend right before the big meet up, you go out and buy a new pair of jeans, shirt, hat, etc. The newer you perceive them to be, the larger the rush of confidence will be.

To recap, buying new clothes for yourself does two very important things:

Forces her to see you in a fresh, unexplored light.

Temporarily skyrockets your confidence level.

Some Quick Fashion Tips

Make sure your nails are always clean and trimmed. This is one of the first things a woman will notice on a man. She'll notice your fingernails long before she sees the brand of watch you're wearing.

Buy a tongue scraper and use it. Your tongue is the source of bad breath and bad breath is just disgusting.

I see lots of guys wearing clothes way too big for their bodies. I suspect this is an attempt to hide body fat. In reality, this actually makes you look bigger. When you reach your arms toward the ceiling, you should be able to see your belly button. If you can't, then your shirt is much too baggy.

Try to make sure all of your clothes work together style wise. You don't want to look like a rock star one day and a DJ the next. It's important to pick a "style" that matches your core personality and stick with it.

Some clothes never go out of style: Leather jacket, black blazer, jeans. It's good to have these in your wardrobe.

Go to a tailor and have him take your correct measurements. Mark them on a business card and shove it in your wallet. It'll come in handy someday – trust me.

Watch the eyebrows! Absolutely no unibrows! Have your eyebrows plucked and shaped if you have to. Go to a salon if need be.

Get a tan! Having a tan can bring up your attractiveness level by as much as 20%. For that reason, it's definitely worth looking into!

Make sure your pubs are always trimmed. Bush is gross on women so it goes without saying it's also gross on guys.

Thou shalt trim all nose hairs. Nose hair is unbelievably disgusting. It's almost as disgusting as bad breath.

Make sure your belt and shoes match. For some reason, women always notice when a guy has matching shoes + belt. Try it and find out.

The more layers you wear, the more "put together" you will look. A sweater with a button up shirt underneath for example.

Layers are good.

A pair of nice shoes is a must. Shoes are the first thing a woman notices on a man, according to studies.

Something I personally love to do is dress down items of clothing that is considered formal. A blazer with blue denim jeans for example.

Go get one expensive haircut. The stylist will shape your hair according to your facial structure and other features. Once done, take a few pictures from all angles and get it duplicated at a less expensive place. Just show them the pictures and you're good.

Avoid black dress shoes. They look better in brown.

If you're a dressy / formal type guy, go out and buy something more relaxed and casual. You need to mix it up a little. Likewise, if you're a casual type of guy, go buy something dressy.

Go test out a ton of colognes. Don't just spray them on test paper and smell them, ask for samples and take them home with you. Try each out and go with the one that suits you the most.

Most guys don't know you can get free samples of cologne.

How long do women take to get ready? They do this all to look good for you. Now, how long do you take to get ready? Consider putting more time into looking good and it will get noticed immediately.

Don't ever brag about how much effort you put into looking good. Make it seem almost effortless. Brush off compliments with a simple "thank you".

There is no doubt that naturally good looking guys have it a bit easier than everyone else. However, there is a big difference between being good looking and looking good. Looking good is by far enough. Don't fall into the trap of thinking all women will only date studs.

You see women every single day with guys not even half as good looking as themselves. This is because (as I stated earlier) women are heavily attracted to the way a man behaves. If he is a so-called "alpha male", he has little to worry about when it comes to attracting women.

THE BIG MEET UP

R ule number one here is not to think of this "meet up" as a date. Don't call it a date and don't have any specific agenda in mind. You're just going to meet up with your ex-girlfriend and see where that takes you. Let things progress naturally without putting any pressure on her to fool around with you or commit to anything romantic/sexual.

You basically want to continue doing what it is you've been doing so far. You want to maintain a cheerful, happy vibe and don't appear angry, depressed, etc. We've talked about all that before so I'm assuming you get the point by now.

Never verbalize what it is you are doing. Don't tell her (or hint toward) you want to get back together. Your job is to simply be an attractive guy and let her worry about where the relationship goes. When you start pulling her in and actively try to get her to date you again, she will naturally push you away. Ideally, you want her pulling you in (chasing you).

Arguments and disagreements are a no-no. The vast majority of times this can be accomplished through not talking about or bringing up your relationship. If she brings it up, fine, go with it. However, you must never under any circumstances be the one to bring up the relationship or any past problems you may have had. Do not place blame on your ex-girlfriend (this will cause her defences to go up). Just be cool about everything.

The Three "C's"

   1. Conversation – When you meet up, you want it to be in a place that's naturally conductive of conversation. So that means the movies are out. Besides, you don't want the "meet up" to smell like a date, and the movies definitely reek of "date".

Being able to converse is important because it is conductive
of building a connection. When you and your ex finally
meet up, she's more than likely going to want to repair the
lost connection and bridge the gap you created with No
Contact.

2.   **Convenient** – It must be convenient for the both of you.
Especially for you. You don't want to demonstrate that
you're going out of your way just to accommodate her.
That's a pretty big "pull" and one you want to avoid
at all costs.

3.   **Cheap** – You don't want it costing loads of money. This
will put pressure on you to pay (especially if that's what
you're used to doing) and that is again another big "pull".
Paying is a huge sign that says "I want to date you". Even if
that's what you really want, you can't convey it until she
herself brings it up.

So the movies are a no-no, dinner costs too much and a vacation to
Hawaii is definitely not convenient. So what does that leave?

Shopping (my all time favourite)

Coffee

Movie at your place or hers (another favourite of mine)

If at all possible, make sure the location is also conductive of a
good time. When you add "adventure" into the equation, it really
puts the power of the "Meet Up" after No Contact on steroids.
Trust me.

The Platonic Vibe

Pay close attention – this part is very
important.

As I mentioned in Chapter 2, you will use a "platonic vibe" to sneak in under the radar and re-build your lost attraction. A platonic vibe means you will hang out as though you are both old friends. Platonic means non-sexual; ie: friends.

If she seems sceptical about meeting up, you can always mention that you believe the breakup was for the best and you look forward to just

being friends. Agreeing that the breakup was a good thing destroys her defences and any resistance she may have to meet you.

You basically want to hang out with your ex girlfriend "as friends" while displaying the traits of an attractive man and ridding yourself of any negative traits you possessed in the past. Please refer back to Chapter 1 of this eBook and Chapter 6 of the Train Your Girlfriend manual. Displaying these traits to your ex-girlfriend is absolutely critical, as it will rapidly re-build attraction with her.

Remember that your advantage lies in the fact that you and your ex already have a strong connection. Another guy cannot just swoop in and build massive amounts of comfort and/or connection with her. This is why I say you should not worry about other men.

The connection is not what you lost (which is why coming in under the radar as friends work wonders). You lost attraction and that is what you must focus on by displaying the traits discussed back in Chapter 1 (and Chapter 6 of TYG).

Note: Agreeing that the breakup was for the best is one of the best things you can do.

Try saying something along the lines of:

"I just wanted to tell you that you were right… The breakup was for the best. It would really be a shame to throw away our friendship though.

Be The Guy In Command!

You now know that women are heavily attracted to men who lead. This is why you need to have a general plan of action when you meet up. Don't ask her what she wants to do, but instead, you want to already know. That doesn't mean you have to plan out every little detail, just know where you're going, how you're both getting there, etc.
Be the guy in command.

For example, if she tells you she thinks you should both get together some time, say: "Alright, sounds good. I have to pick up a new pair of jeans at the mall, so we should go there. It'll be fun. How does that sound?"

She'll likely agree, at which point you can always tell her you'll pick her up at a specific time (you recommend a time that's good for you). If she's busy and that particular time doesn't work for her, recommend another time that's good for the both of you. Be accommodating, but not overly so. You want to come across as though you would like to see her again, but you're not desperate to see her.

Pick her up, drive to the mall, lead her into a few different stores. Joke around and have a fun time together. Talk about upbeat, fun, positive things. You never want to nag and bring up the past (in a negative way). Basically, you don't want her thinking about the bad times you had together. If you can manage to leave the bad out, she'll automatically only focus on the good.

STEPS SEDUCTION

Believe it or not, the reason you got "lucky" with your girlfriend (the first time) and landed all those dates which eventually lead to a relationship is because of the way in which you presented yourself to her. It was how you subconsciously communicated all the traits we talked about in the above chapters.

I'm going to teach you a potent 4-step seduction process that will skyrocket your ex girlfriends attraction toward you. Another benefit to this 4-step seduction process is that it will work on virtually any woman. It doesn't have to be your ex-girlfriend. Keep that in mind for any future women you may consider dating!

Step #1: Art of the Tease

Forget what you think you know about flirting. Flirting =

Teasing. All the rules that once applied in kindergarten,

apply once again!

Once you've completed all the other steps and you've landed the meet up by presenting yourself as the man you once were (confident, secure, etc), it's now time to lay on the attraction techniques.

You must assume the attitude that you're slightly cooler than her. I'm not talking about being condescending, ignorant or rude – just slightly cooler. Kind of like you would view a little sister. That's the mentality I want you to have. She's kind of like your dorky little sister.

With a big smile on your face, chuckle and call her a dork if she does something embarrassing. Do it in a joking tone – if you can't find that balance it will come across as cocky (which signals insecurity).

I always recommend that you give her a flirtatious nickname:

Munchkin
Kitten
Pumpkin
Muffin Head

Those are merely generic, non-specific nicknames. If you can, make the nickname as specific to her as you possibly can. For example, you might call her "polka dots" because she's wearing a polka dot shirt.

I always look for something that stands out on a girl – something unique and unusual and then I find a way to playfully make fun of it. Do not confuse playfully making fun of something with insulting her.

You also don't want to overdo any one specific tease. You don't want to be calling her "polka dots" every ten minutes. It'll be funny for the first few times but after that use it sparingly and find other things to tease her about.

You're basically either poking fun at her mild insecurities or making her feel mildly insecure about something (such as her shoes, shirt, haircut). The key do doing this effectively is to make sure the insecurities are very mild.

This technique is absolute gold when done correctly. It's important to realize that you cannot pick something she is genuinely insecure about. If the women you're pocking fun at is a little overweight, don't call her chubby whatever you do! The goal here is not to insult, but to demonstrate you're a confident, playful guy who likes to have fun.

You can poke fun at her shoes, hair, a funky outfit she

has on. The possibilities are literally endless. As long as you come across as non-insulting, you're safe. I see a lot of guys mess up on this one, by coming across as insulting. You should do this with a big smile on your face that shows you are only being playful.

Reverse Statement of Intent (SOI)

This is where you reverse sexual intent roles. Basically pretend she is hitting on you.

So when are you taking me out for dinner polka dots? You know, I'm pretty high maintenance. I expect you to take me to all the best restaurants, and buy me ALL the best food... in a limo of course. :)"

"What kind of guy do you think I am? I'm not just going to take you home and give you mind numbing orgasms and non-stop adventure for nothing you know. You have to buy me at least a few drinks first!
:)"

Being Over-The-Top

I love being dramatic when interacting with women. If she hits me, I'll put a shocked look on my face and say "OUCH!" really loud then give her a playful shove. Playfully overreact to things that happen during your interaction.

Positive Energy (Happiness)

This is the most important of all the attraction tools I use. It's not even so much a technique, as a mindset, but I believe it to be of the utmost importance when generating attraction with women. As a general rule, be 15% or 20% above her energy level.

Make sure you're in a positive, upbeat mood. Not just around hot women, but around EVERYONE. Happiness is

ADDICTIVE. When I'm with a woman, I focus on having a great time first and foremost. I make sure I'm having a blast because I know that if I'm having a great time, so will she, by association.

Mood transferring is a very real phenomenon. If you're around somebody who happens to be in a very bad mood, it will almost always rub off on you. The same applies to positive energy. The more positive energy she feels while with you, the better.

Having a positive, upbeat mindset is very conductive of flirting and teasing. In other words, if you can just concentrate on having a great time, you won't even need to focus on flirting and teasing. It will happen much more naturally.

Step #2: Kino

Kino stands for kinesthetic, which means "touch" in normal people speak. It's absolutely imperative that she become comfortable with your touch, early on in your interaction.

Incidental Kino

Incidental kino will be easy for you specifically because you already are physically comfortable with each other (Hello! You slept together). The point I want to highlight though, is that you can't keep your distance from her, which would just make things awkward between the two of you, eventually.

Think back to some of the most awkward dates you had with women. I'm willing to bet money it was because there was no "incidental kino" to make her comfortable with you. The power of touch is amazing!

With that said, I'm not recommending you hang off her! That would be completely counter to the non-needy, secure man I have been prepping you to be through this eBook. Just don't be afraid to touch her in a masculine, secure way.

Note: Never look at your hand when touching her. It's subtly seeking permission.

Direct Kino

Full Front Hug
Holding Hands
Arm in arm escorting
Massage

Step #3: Taking Things to the Next Level

If you're doing everything right up to this point, then there is little doubt in my mind that your ex will be overtly finding "excuses" to touch you and she'll also be teasing you too. That's a great sign!

At this point, you really need to gauge her body language. The rule of thumb here is not to put any more energy into the interaction than she does. You don't want to work any harder or show any more affection than she is.

You know she's being very receptive to your teasing if she starts lightly hitting you on the arm telling you to "stop" while giggling. If you can get that sort of reaction out of her, you're "in"!

The second sign I look for is the "tranquilizer gaze". This is basically when she stares at you then looks at your lips and then licks or pouts her lips. If she does this, she is sending you a clear signal to "KISS ME!".

Typically, when I'm with a woman, I will gradually amp up the kino throughout the interaction. Of course I'll start small with playfully pinching her cheeks or giving her a playful shove when she does something stupid (and I'll call her a dork at the same time).

I'll progress until she's either on my couch or my bed and I'm tickling her or giving her a massage (direct kino). If she's letting you tickle her and she's laughing and having a great time, you can kiss her without fear of rejection. After the tickle progression, I've never been rejected.

Also, if you decide to give her a massage, you will know to kiss her when she slightly tilts her head to the side. Women are always indirect. They just expect up guys to pick up on these subtleques. In reality, none of us really pick up on them.

As opposed to just jumping into a kiss, I like to breathe in her ear, gently bite it, smell her hair (women find that immensely attractive!) Once you're getting away with all that, it's really just a matter of tilting her head slightly toward yours and kissing her.

A lot of the time, you will find it will be your ex-girlfriend initiating the kiss, provided you pumped her up enough with teasing and playful kino.

Miscellaneous Tip

If you're at her place and not yours, spray a tiny bit of your cologne on her bathroom towel or bedroom pillow (if you think you can get away with it without being caught). Obviously only spray a bit on – anything more and you'll arouse suspicion. The sent will remind her of you and seriously cause her to miss you. Women are more stimulated by smell than us men.

CASE STUDY

y best friend Brian was pretty bummed out after his girlfriend broke up with him. They had been in a relationship for almost 9 months when she dropped the bomb. It still hit him like a ton of bricks even though he was half expecting it.

Like most guys, Brian "sensed" something was up but really didn't understand why or what to do to make things right again. He was literally completely lost. He didn't even come to me (his best friend) until it was too late. She had already broken up with him.

His story was one I had heard a million times before. Slowly his girlfriend started losing interest in him. She wouldn't call him as much, her tone of voice seemed different, she got annoyed at the smallest things and she didn't laugh at his jokes. Overall, Brian felt pretty bad about himself. His self esteem was slowly being shot to pieces.

When he finally came to me for help, his confidence was a total mess. I made him explain everything to me; and I mean everything. I wanted to get to the root cause of the breakup. I knew that even though she had told Brian she "just needed space" there was a deeper reason. There always is.

As I suspected, Brian had developed a needy, approval seeking mind-set which was the root cause of his girlfriend's loss of attraction for him. For starters, he put way too much effort into the relationship.

Remember: "He who cares least, controls the relationship."
When they first started dating, Brian described it as "she was the one pursuing me". Brian was the one with the "power" and his

girlfriend essentially followed his lead. Somewhere along the line, the "male/female" polarity (as I call it) shifted. His girlfriend began assuming a more dominant role while Brian became more and more submissive.

I explained to Brian that this was quite natural. Women are actually hardcoded to "test" men and continually push the boundaries of a relationship. It wasn't really her fault as she had no conscious control over it. She literally had to do it.

What Brian should have done was to maintain his dominance and not give in to her bratty behaviour. He should have put his foot down and made it clear from the very beginning that he would not put up with her lack of respect. See the chapter on punishing bad behaviour in the "Train Your Girlfriend" manual.

Unfortunately, that's not what he did. He gave in to her unreasonable demands and slowly began to put her needs far ahead of his own. To women, this is weak behaviour and they will lose attraction rapidly once they have taken control of the relationship. At this point, she no longer seemed interested in sex or any type of intimate encounter. Pretty common stuff I hear about all the time.

You see, once a woman has essentially turned her mate into a "beta male", she will lose attraction, stop having sex with him and either break up with him or cheat on him with an "alpha male". Now, I know Brian and I know that when they first started going out, he was definitely the "alpha male" and it saddened me to see him change so much. I had to be brutally honest with him. I had to tell it like it was, even if it meant hurting his feeling. I knew it was for his own good.

I explained to Brian that he had to take back control and present himself as the "high value" guy he once was. I sat him down and made him compare the man he once was (in the relationship) to the man he had become, months later. That was a real revelation for Brian. It really hit him. He admitted that he was no longer the fun-loving, spontaneous guy he used to be.

As he thought about it more and more, Brian realized he had slowly become more and more insecure. He would lash out at his girlfriend for talking with other guys, ask where she was and who she was with all the time and generally be the "overly protective boyfriend".

I could see it in his eyes; he suddenly knew why she no longer wanted to be with him.

Then came the hard part. How the heck could he turn things around? How could he "re-attract" her?

I told him this wasn't actually the hard part at all. He needed to stop contacting her and wait until she initiated contact with him. He needed to use this time to re-connect with his masculine, attractive side and work on building up his self-esteem so he could be secure with himself once again.

The first step he took was to take all of his ex's things and put them in a box. He was going to put the box under his bed but I made him stash it at my place instead. This way I was sure he wouldn't get drunk one night, look through her things and call her up crying. That would just be devastating. So the box went under my bed.

Next, Brian and I hit the mall. He knew how to dress fairly well as it was but that wasn't really the point. I wanted him to feel "new" and "fresh". New clothes always make a person feel 10 times as confident, especially if their great looking clothes. As for working out, I urged him to start going to the gym. Turns out he actually wanted an excuse to get back in shape. The only bad news was he wanted me to join with him. Mr I'm-a-lazy-bastard-and-never-get-off-my-butt. Oh well, I figured I'd do it for my best friend.

That night we called up a bunch of our friends and went out together. I have to admit I was happy to have Brian back "in the game". I missed the old times we used to have, just him and I, partying all night. I could tell he was actually looking at things in a more positive light now, and maybe even missed those times too.

I made sure to invite a few of the girls I knew out, so Brian could get used to flirting again. Turns out one of the girls liked him quite a bit. I was happy to hear they had also arranged for a date. Nice.

As you can imagine, Brian was pretty happy. His self esteem shot through the roof, but I knew he still needed to actually convey the confidence and self-worth to his ex-girlfriend. The next night we all went out, I made sure to bring my digital camera along and took a bunch of pictures. Brian and his ex both had Facebook so I posted them on his account. There were a few pics of this new "mystery girl" sitting on Brian's lap. His ex-was sure to see them and get rather jealous.

And as always, I was right. It was going on a little over a week since Brian initiated No Contact and she finally caved that weekend. She called him up, acting all innocent, asking what he was up to. Brian didn't take that as an opportunity to brag, he just brushed it off and said he was spending time out with "the guys". Then she asked if he wanted to hang out, to which he agreed. "Sure," he said, "I'm picking up a new pair of jeans, you could help me look for something nice."

Atta boy Brian, just what I told him to say. And she quickly agrees.

The next day when he picked her up, he had a general plan of action in mind. He led her around through each store looking for a nice pair of jeans. They laughed and generally had a great time together. Everything was going smooth. Brian didn't act angry, upset and he didn't talk about the relationship whatsoever. He just hung out with her as if she were a close friend.

After they left the mall, she asked "so what do you want to do now?" and Brian quickly replied with "you know, I'm pretty hungry, how about a bite to eat?" She agrees and so he drove over to Boston Pizza.

Now, Brian didn't give me too many details as to what happened after that but rest assured they both ended up at his place and I'll leave the rest to your imagination. They worked things out and are still together as I write this. The main reason for that is Brian realized he needed to "man up" and take charge of the relationship.

Since Brian's breakup, I've developed many other techniques that I shared with you in previous chapters. Put your thinking cap on and use them all to your advantage.

MAKEUP SEX

I know most guys don't want to be given tips on how to be better in bed, but I honestly couldn't exclude this chapter. Put your ego aside for a moment and listen to what I have to say because I'm going to give you some pretty solid tips and tricks on how to get more pleasure for yourself as well as for your girl.

I've always been a believer in that women absolutely love sex. Maybe your past girlfriends tried to manipulate you with sex and only gave it to you when you were on your best behaviour. If you ask me, that's bullshit. You should be the one in charge of when you have sex; and if you're good in bed, you will be.

Women actually have orgasms ten times more powerful then men do. Jealous? I certainly am. That's still pretty good news for you though because if you can be the one to provide her with mind-numbing orgasms again and again, you'll be getting sex whenever you want it. She will basically want it more than you do.

Dominance

Dominance is by far the number one thing you can bring to bed with you. Women want a take-charge man when it comes to sex (and anything really). Women want to be told what to do, when to do it and even how to do it.

Physically dominate her by moving her into the positions you want.

Tell her when she's doing something you like.

Moan or grunt when she's doing something you like.

Talk dirty to her, which is a personal favorite of mine (see below)

Some women even go so far to imagine themselves as animals. There's just something about animalistic sex that really turns them on.

Your #1 Most Powerful Tool In The Bedroom

Your voice is your #1 tool in the bedroom. That's right, your voice. To be more specific, it's what you say and how you exert your dominance with your voice. You use your voice to tell her what you want her to do for you, what you're about to do to her and you use your voice to say naughty things.

Most guys are actually pretty quiet in bed. They just huff and puff until they finish. Bad idea. You can do way better than that.

I remember back to my first long-term girlfriend. She absolutely loved to be "animalistic" in bed. The more I talked dirty to her, the crazier she went, in multi-orgasmic bliss.

I'd tell her how naughty she was, how slutty I wanted her to be and how wet she was. The first couple of times it took a great deal of courage. I'd swallow hard and blurt out another raunchy line. She loved it! Every freakin' time.

I believe it's the mental stimulation that makes dirty talk so powerful. While men are aroused by visual imagery, women take pleasure in sound, touch and feeling. Women want to feel like a slut in bed. Unfortunately, most guys are too timid or suffer from limiting (religious?) beliefs to even attempt to try this.

A lot of guys are concerned that they will insult their girlfriends if they talk dirty to them. First of all, women like it when you say dirty things to them in bed. Remember that. Secondly, I would recommend easing into it. Start off by saying "small" dirty things and gauge her reaction. I guarantee she will like it. Use this to build your confidence up to the point where you're saying you want her to act like a slut.

PREVENTING ANOTHER BREAKUP

T he vast majority of those of you currently reading this will have already gone through a breakup. However, a few of you will have purchased this program in anticipation of your looming breakup. Either way, everyone reading this will benefit in some way or another.

The power of this technique can and will come in handy someday in the future. Having the peace of mind in knowing exactly how to handle a looming breakup is (without question) a huge weight off your shoulders.

Now, first let me start by saying that this technique is not 100% effective. Nothing is - and if anyone claims to have all the answers they are either lying or trying to sell you something. Period.

Let's begin.

The Technique...

Preventing a breakup as it happens is actually pretty easy. We can all "sense" when a woman is losing attraction for us. They stop looking at us with the same loving eyes. They pick fights with us for seemingly no reason at all. They stop giving us sex. You know the way it goes. We've all been there.

It all culminates until she gives you "the talk". She'll usually start it off by saying "we need to talk" or something along those lines. Or perhaps she'll spontaneously break up with you after picking a staged fight; using the fight as justification for the breakup itself.

The trick (much like everything else you've read in my other books) is very counter-intuitive.

The big secret is that you need to agree with her decision. Or, if you know she's just about to give you the axe, you can tell her to break up with you. I know, I know… it's scary stuff. Even for me, it would be scary. We fear the unknown.

In the Train Your Girlfriend manual I talk about a concept called "walking power". Women are attracted to and respect men who are willing to walk away if their integrity is compromised. The same factors apply here.

If she believes you're fine with the breakup, you've managed to maintain a position of integrity. Or at least you will not have compromised it anywhere near that of any other man. Most men react by begging, pleading and even crying in some cases. That type of behaviour certainly doesn't aid in flicking any attraction switches – that's for sure.

I'll give you some examples as to what to say (just as she's about to break up with you):

"Lana, you're a great girl. You make me smile. You really do. But maybe I'm not the right guy for you? Maybe you need to break up with me if that's what your heart is telling you?"

Or, if she's clearly telling you she wants to break up with you:

"You know, you're probably right. You have to do what your heart tells you. If I'm not the guy for you then I'm not the guy for you. I obviously like you and all, but that's life I guess. Even if it sucks, that's just the way it is."

Don't come across as bitter or hateful when you say the above. Don't act aloof and like you don't care either! Simply say it in a light-hearted manner. Assume the mentality that she's a great girl, but you can live your life without her. Either way, life will go on.

It's important that you do not break up with her first. Even though it might seem like the right thing to do based on what you've learned in the Train Your Girlfriend manual. If you break up with her first, the burden will be on you to pursue her and initiate contact. No Contact is an important role within this whole guide and it won't be nearly as effective if you are the one doing the dumping. The dynamic totally changes.

That is why telling her (nicely) to break up with you is very effective. Stick closely to the script above and you'll be fine. However, try to understand the underlying meaning and reason behind the words. You're basically telling her that she's a great girl (you like her) and that if her heart isn't in it then it's fine to end things. No hard feelings.

This dynamic totally throws her off. It's nowhere near how she expects you to react/behave.

If She Agrees And Goes Forward With The Breakup Anyway…

I also must warn you that she may agree with you at first and actually go forward with the breakup. She will probably be hesitant about it but perhaps she may still go forward and agree the breakup is for the best. Don't panic, this is fine.

You've managed to at least save your dignity and self-respect in her eyes. Even if she goes forward with the breakup (still) you can be certain she will be shaken and confused by your reaction. Combine this technique with No Contact and you're almost certain to get her back. Throw in a little jealousy plotline and I honestly can't see this working for just about anyone.

Other Preventative Measures…

If you know that a breakup is only a few days away, you want to get both of your adrenaline pumpings. That means you need to plan an adventure and both have massive fun together. Adrenaline with help the both of you to rapidly re-bond.

This is not a permanent solution. If the root of the probably is not solved, with will only delay things. Reading the Train Your Girlfriend manual will help you understand what female attraction is (and how it is different). It'll also give you specific advice on how to behave in an attractive way while in a relationship.

Some "adventure" ideas are as follows:

Go on a vacation to an exotic resort. The new surrounding will be exciting and fresh. It'll give you ample opportunity to reignite lost attraction by demonstrating the "traits of an attractive man" (discussed in the Train Your Girlfriend manual).

Amusement park. If this doesn't get your adrenaline pumping then nothing will.

Rock climbing.

Laser tag / arcade

Break The Routine…

Break out of the boring routine you and your girlfriend have built up over the months/years. Couples get comfortable and this comfort kills attraction. It's boring and stale. Unfortunately, we don't really realize this until it's too late. I'm giving you a head start here.

SUMMARY

Congratulations on finishing this book. You're well on your way to getting your ex-girlfriend back already. Most men will <u>never</u> come to know what you now know. Take pride in that.

Even though at this moment you're not yet back with your girlfriend. You have within you the knowledge and abilities too put forth these newly learnt techniques and methods.

I strongly urge you to start reading the "Train Your Girlfriend Manual" right this second. I can guarantee you it will help you get back with your girlfriend. A lot of the advice in that eBook is very transferable to what you are now going through.

By reading the "Train Your Girlfriend" manual, you'll no longer have to guess at why your relationship went south. It's not a traditional relationship book, so you won't find any lovey-dovey nonsense. I expose to you what it is women really want. Much of the information is far from politically correct.

ULTIMATE CHEAT SHEET GUIDE

These are the extremely helpful reference pages, strongly recommend keeping a copy of these during dates and meet ups.

CHEAT SHEET

This guide is broken down into 6 distinct phases:

1. Understanding why your ex dumped you.

2. Ending contact with your ex until she contacts you first.

3. Ridding yourself of neediness and insecurity.

4. Creating a "fear of loss" within your ex-girlfriend.

5. The big meet up.

6. Makeup sex.

FEMALE ATTRACTION

- Women are attracted to the way a man **behaves** much more than physical "looks", money or fame. Of course those things will help, but behaving in an attractive, masculine manner will be more than necessary.

- Insecurity and acting "needy" repel women like nothing else. These behaviours are interpreted as weak and turn women off, sexually.

- Traits of a dominant, attractive man are:

o Leadership (always have a plan, know what you're doing, where you're going, etc)
o Confidence (be secure in yourself, don't be afraid to speak your mind, do what makes **you** happy above everything else)
o Self-Assurance (Be sure of yourself, assertive, pursue that which makes you happy as opposed to just making your girlfriend happy)
- **Women do not want the "power" in a relationship.** They are only attracted to men who take charge and lead them. This does not mean to start being controlling, it means to start leading more and being more dominant / less submissive.

- **He who cares least, controls the relationship.** Whoever has the most feeling and emotion invested in the relationship will subconsciously communicate that and thus push their partner away. Typically men who care *too much* will begin
Acting needy and insecure.

• Picture the man you were when you first started dating your girlfriend. Now, picture the man you became. Did the "male/female" polarity shift and you started to act more submissive while your girlfriend assuming a dominant role?

NO CONTACT

- Do not initiate contact with your ex-girlfriend. Wait until she initiates contact with you first.

- "No Contact" will instil a **fear of loss** within her, keep you from acting **needy and insecure** and give you time to read over this material.

- Most women keep their ex boyfriends around as "friends" to help themselves heal. While the ex-boyfriend is around giving his ex-girlfriend emotional support, who is there to support the boyfriend?

- If she contacts you, make it appear as though you have already moved on with your life. Appear as though you're perfectly fine with the breakup. Generally act happy and cheerful.

- Women experience massive loneliness after **three to four weeks** of No Contact. She will be at her most vulnerable at this point. If you decide to contact her at this point, she will be very receptive.

PUSH/PULL THEORY

- A "pull" is when you demonstrate interest and show affection. A "push" as the opposite; it is when you demonstrate disinterest and lack affection.

- **We pursue that which retreats from us.** If you "pull" too much, your ex-girlfriend will retreat from you and generally have her guard up. If you push (just a bit), your ex will feel a fear of loss (she can't have you) and pursue you instead.
  Riding Yourself of Neediness & Insecurity

- Delete your ex-girlfriends number from your phone.

- Remove all pictures of her from your house.

- Get rid of anything at all that reminds you of her.
- Build confidence by working out, buying new cloths for yourself, surrounding yourself with happy, positive people.

- Never view her online profile. Facebook, Instagram, Snapchat, etc. Resist the urge and NEVER VIEW HER PROFILE.

- Concentrate only on the negative aspects of your girlfriend.

- Visualize yourself with other women. Do not fantasize about your ex-girlfriend under any circumstances.

CREATING A FEAR OF LOSS WITHIN YOUR EX

- Start dating other women. Word gets around and your ex is sure to hear about it. Clearly this will make her jealous.

- Make your nickname on any instant messaging system "on a date, back later". This will ensure your ex finds out.

- Flirt with other women on social networking sites like Facebook. She'll see that you're not dwelling on her and want you back.

- Take pictures of yourself with other women and post them online.

- Generally appear as though you have moved on with your life and you no longer *need* your ex-girlfriend.

MEETING UP WITH YOUR EX

- Have a plan of action. Be the guy in commend. Know where you're going, demonstrate leadership, lead the way.

- Remember the three C's. Conversation, Convenient, Cheap. Shopping, watching a movie at your place, going out for coffee are all great "meet up" locations.

  Do not bring up or mention any type of past relationship problems.

  Do not ask if she's dating or sleeping with another guy.

  Generally be happy, positive and cheerful. This will keep you from appearing needy or insecure.

THE ULTIMATE GUIDE

HOW TO WIN BACK YOUR EX